joyful spirit bubbling

faith and spirit through the seasons

bronwyn angela white

Philip
Garside
Publishing Ltd.

www.spiritandfaithwords.com

Also by Bronwyn Angela White:
You who delight me • Something new to say

Signs of home, Suddenly there is light all around and *You who delight* me previously published in 'You who delight me,' Steele Roberts Aotearoa, 2012

Cover design and photograph
© Bronwyn Angela White

Author photo © Warwick Metcalfe

Paperback International edition 2024
ISBN 9781991027580

Also available
New Zealand paperback: ISBN 9781991027597
Paperback print-on-demand USA: ISBN 9798864717004

PDF: ISBN 9781991027566
ePub: ISBN 9781991027573

Philip Garside Publishing Ltd
PO Box 17160
Wellington 6147
Aotearoa New Zealand

www.philipgarsidebooks.com

books@pgpl.co.nz

Contents

About the words.. 5

Summer in Aotearoa.. 6
Blessings that blossom in our lives................................7
Drama of our lives 8
Gifts of other faiths and cultures 9
Joyful Spirit bubbling...10

Autumn in Aotearoa 11
An evolving response...12
Your stories tell our lives..13
Autumn Benediction..14
Celebrating mothers and women of mana....................15

Winter in Aotearoa 16
Journeys, homecoming, manaakitanga........................17
Blessing for Winter Meal 19
Prayers for Family 20
Raindrops pizzicato 22
Prayers on Father's Day 23

Spring in Aotearoa 24
Aotearoa Spring—prayers of pavement and city square....25
We are blessed with enough..26
Botanical Gardens prayers...27
With the Spring comes the greening..............................29
Sometimes Spring..30
Vigour of rain and passion of sunshine 31

Seasons in one day 32

Reflections and essays.......................................33
Allies or Traitors...33
Blessed be the work of our hands..................................38
Feast in the wilderness (i): Next year in Jerusalem.................43
Feast in the wilderness (ii): The Promised Land....................44
Loving Boldly—What makes a leader?............................. 45

3

Milk from the breast of Christ 50

Put on your glad rags and break the rules!............................51

Sacred stones and sites—reflection and liturgy 58

Voices of the deep 63

Affirmations, prayers, blessings 68

Blessings of Greenness.. 69

Affirmation of Faith (ii): Come, let us walk the road.............. 69

Litany for departing 70

Walls, Gates and Tables..70

Trees blessing... 71

Glossary and References 72

Glossary 73

Bibliography and sources... 74

Thanks... 75

Also by bronwyn angela white 76

About the words

"Joyful Spirit Bubbling" follows the seasons in Aotearoa New Zealand, starting with summer—December, January, February—and moving through Autumn and Winter to end with the revival and hope of Spring. But there are poems, prayers and reflections that don't sit within a particular season or theme: these are my offerings for Ordinary Time.

Several pieces were written as litanies, with 'the leader' beginning each section and 'the people' responding with the lines in italics.

Most of the resources in this book were written to be read aloud as part of a service of worship. There are a couple of exceptions, extracts from essays written for a Religious Studies paper I took at Victoria University of Wellington in the summer semester of 2000-2001.

With a working title of *Spirit through the seasons,* I intended this book to follow both the liturgical and calendar years. However, I had too much material for a single slim volume, so the liturgical year resources—relating to "high days and holy days"—will be published in a fourth book.

I hope these resources will be enjoyed and shared by anyone who sees the sacred in the everyday.

Copyright and usage

You are welcome to use with acknowledgement—and if necessary, slightly adapt for the occasion—all this liturgical material.

Summer in Aotearoa

December, January, February

Blessings that blossom in our lives

We invite into our hearts and lives
—the Flourishing Spirit of growth and expansiveness,
of manaakitanga—hospitality and celebration
the Liberating Spirit of compassion and empathy,
murunga hara—forgiving others and ourselves
letting go of hurts and regrets,
restoring others' mana, creating mana ōrite;
and the Wairua of perception, clear-sightedness,
mōhiotanga—insight and knowing, seeing the God-ness in others,
treating and Treaty-ing as we would be treated, keeping faith.

We wait in the quiet of this whare karakia for the gift of insight into the hearts of others, and the reassurances we each need.

We celebrate the many blessings that blossom in our lives:
small benedictions of kind words and pleasant company,
natural wonders, the spark of solidarity
when discovering a shared sense of humour,
finding the exact change needed when you're late for the bus,
the unguarded smile of a child, the perfection of moss on a stone.

In over 80 countries, World Religion Day is celebrated today, to foster interfaith understanding and harmony.

We recognise the common elements underlying all religions and faiths, the golden rule of treating others as we would be treated in their place.

On this day when we celebrate the diversity of faiths,
we think too of the people around the world
whose dreams and achievements are destroyed
by natural disasters, civil war and heartless political decisions.

As we go from the safety of this whare karakia
 gifted with insight into the hearts of others,
whose needs for reassurance are so like our own,
we no longer wait, but claim the flourishing, liberation,
perception that's already ours.

Drama of our lives

We give thanks that grace is waiting in the wings
to prompt us when we forget our part in the drama
of our life together.

When our lives feel like a gag reel, and we dwell on the out-takes,
the spluttering and mistakes, we give thanks for friends or strangers
who remind us that they see our lives as things of beauty.

We give thanks for the gracious spirits who know our intent,
who edit our misconceptions and perspective,
leaving past misjudgements on the cutting room floor
of forgiveness and reconciliation and show us at our best.

We give thanks for those who share good news
on stage and screen, from lectern or laptop,
via internet and intentional conversation.

For the talents of writing and scripting and editing,
for lyrics and libretto, for melody and harmony, grace notes and
counterpoint, for comedy with depth and lightly delivered,
serious sermons, we give thanks.

For those who sing and preach and entertain,
for the choreography and charism of our liturgy,
for those who collect our garbage and sort our recycling,
for those who repurpose and reuse and reconcile and redeem,
we give thanks.

When we forget the Benevolent Force behind things, and feel afraid,
may we act the part of a Loving Companion
until we become that friend
say words of kindness and healing to help others,
until they come alive in us.

May we play our part, our many parts, until they become real:
imagining, creating and living the Commonwealth of Peace.

Gifts of other faiths and cultures

World Religion Day

We celebrate the gifts of other faiths and cultures:
parable and koan,
whakamatau and midrash,
paradox and pun:
for the Koran and the Torah
Vedic Scriptures and Bhagwad Gita
for Korero o Nehera
We give thanks.

We give thanks for the stories of Jesus
of Hagar and Joshua and Eve
of Ruth and Peter and Hannah
of Moses and Saul, Rahab and Beatrice
of Jonathon and Martha.

We give thanks for the storytellers
The wise ones around the fires
The grandmothers perching us on their lap
The uncles or neighbours or schoolteachers
who read to us—fables and poems and folklore,
bible stories and classical myths, or
told us stories from their own imagination.

For Anansi of Ghana, Siddhārtha Gautama of India,
for Lao-Tze and Maimonides
for Isis and Lakshmi and Amaterasu
for Tangaroa and Hine-nui-te-Pō
for storytellers and mythmakers.

For the Creative Spirit in all times and in all peoples
we give thanks.

Joyful Spirit bubbling

Creative Spirit dancing in river and ocean
and summer rain waiting in water urn

Wild Spirit of wilderness, speaking from burning bush,
from tussock and hebe, desert road and city street

Temperate Spirit of national park, green pasture
and market square—speaking in a small voice
or in the crashing of breakers on our shores

Joyful Spirit bubbling in our celebrations,
enlivening people and communities,
rising in our bread and sparkling our wine:

We hold in our hearts those who need our concern,
and for whom justice is still a dream.
We give thanks that our water jars of longing are filled
with the miraculous wine, and filled again to overflowing,
when we go where truth and justice lead.

As we long for justice and work for peace,
we think of our sisters and brothers
of all faiths—and none—who share our concern.

We hold in our hearts homeless people throughout the world:
exiles and asylum seekers,
prophets unrecognised in their own countries,
and all whose journey leads them far from home.
We bless those who have shown us kindness
and made us welcome.

We hold in our hearts all who work for peace and reconciliation,
and all whose efforts to make peace
expose them to attacks from both sides.
We bless all who work for social, racial or religious justice
throughout the world.

We hold in our hearts respect for the natural world
and delight in its wonder and riches,
and those people whose experience of the natural world
has been impoverished through the circumstances of their lives
or the actions of others.
We bless those who help us nurture sensitivity
to the spiritual resonance of nature.

We hold in our hearts: those who ask, "How long?"
—those who wait for truth to rise again.

Autumn in Aotearoa

March, April, May

An evolving response

On reading the media outpourings following Friday's terrorist attacks on mosques in Christchurch—50 killed, many more wounded—on Friday 15 March 2019

I've got the temporary slogan and I've posted of forgiveness
and I've tried to keep myself out of the space of actual victims,
and I have a friend who's Muslim and I'm glad he's in Malaysia
although I'd also like to hug him, and say,
"This is not New Zealand."

Yet I have to ask, would we have said,
"Yes, they are us, of course they are!" last year?

And if someone in shalwar qameez fired on my congregation,
would I feel consoled or terrified, if my church filled up with Muslims,
offering the will of Allah, and strange food, and their emotions—
or would it overwhelm and scare me,
never mind their good intentions?

And will we still be saying, "They are us," next year
when someone in a burkha wants to leave it on in court
and when a turban-wearing guy
sits down beside us with his backpack
and in ten years, when the clothes shops
stock a wide jilbab selection?

And in twenty years when that young boy affected by the trauma
thinks his elders are too soft for their accepting and forgiveness,
when he joins an online group recruiting bruised young men
as radicals—when he's tempted by "Jihad Cool" stuff, and bitter,
will we say, "He's us," and love him?

And I hope the answer's Yes to these and other awkward questions,
and I know we need to act as if forgiveness is the answer,
and we know the way to peace is not through brute retaliation—

But I still find myself asking,
will we say, "They're us—and we are them," next Thursday?

Your stories tell our lives

Post-Christian prayer / hymn lyrics

JESUS, YOUR WORDS, repeated by your friends
retold, reworked, interpreted for ears
unused to midrash, used to meet the ends
of politics, and altered through the years
to build a church you had no mind to found
create a Christ you made no claim to be
still with an own-life in our hearts resound
inspiring us with truths which set us free:
Your stories tell our lives, dare and invite
affirm our shadow-selves and offer light.

JESUS, YOUR DEATH, through ritual mystified
as though some merit from your blood accrued,
transformed as though your being crucified
was an unusual fate; as though imbued
with an unwonted grace; as if some powers
(the sacrificial lamb led to the knife)
led you somehow to a better death than ours,
a martyr's death, exalted over life
Yet still your body, lowered into earth
affirms in us the promise of re-birth.

JESUS, YOUR FRIENDS, awash with guilt and loss
needed to find some meaning in their pain,
found their salvation in an empty cross;
in mourning, shared your life, saw you again:
Your words inspiring them to spread the news,
Your vision showing them that living starts
where love is shared, when power is rightly used,
Your spirit, resurrected in their hearts.
We share our stories, selves; grief, celebration:
affirm through love our powers of re-creation.

Autumn Benediction

As the trees release their leaves
so we let go of those things we need carry no longer.

Go in peace—
into the green and gold, ochre and amber
and crunch of leaves under foot,
your journey bright and pure.

May you find grace in the love of friends, family and community
surprises amid the commonplace
and songs of thanks to fill your heart
this day and always.

Amen.

Celebrating mothers and women of mana

Mothering Spirit, we give thanks for the women and men,
the carers and nurturers who lead by example,
who ask questions about authority and social responsibility,
who make time to dance and sing.

On this day when we celebrate mothers and women of authority,
we hold in our hearts those who lack the confidence and
empowerment that a wise, loving and supportive mother figure
would have given them.

We hold in our hearts parents with illness or disabilities which make
it hard to care for their children in all the ways they might wish;
Mothers with postnatal depression which inhibits the joy and love
that others take for granted
and the partners who love and grieve for them.

We think of mothers struggling without partner, family
or community support
refugee and migrant parents whose lives and networks
have been shattered;
those who lack parenting skills and options
due to inter-generational poverty, family breakdown, or abuse.

We hold them in our hearts, Mothering Spirit,
and offer them our care.
We give thanks for those who care for us
when we are distant from loved families,
for the experienced wisdom of elders
and the innocent wisdom of children.

May Hine-te-iwaiwa, atua of childbirth, weaving and female arts,
exemplary figure of a wife and mother,
inspire us to also care for our Earth Mother, Papatūānuku,
from whose womb all life is born, and for all her tamariki.

Sacred Spirit arouse in us the strength of Miriam
and the courage of Mary. These are our prayers.

Winter in Aotearoa

June, July, August

Journeys, homecoming, manaakitanga

World Refugee Day

Bewildering spirit of paradox and metaphor
We give thanks that our journeys and wilderness experiences,
our searches for meaning and flight from old doctrines
have led us to this place: a place where all are welcome,
a community of faith rather than dogma
to a starting point for new quests or a haven from our lost years
to a place in our lives where we don't need all the answers
yet can ask the awkward questions.

Enlivening Spirit of deep, still waters and crashing waves
May ours be the hands outstretched to greet those who journey
from another place; who leave what's familiar,
to start a new life—whether refugees from distant lands
or neighbours from city and suburbs
whether they have fled from warfare and danger
or from church or family where they no longer feel safe.

Perplexing Spirit of challenge and compassion
We hold in our hearts especially the Muslim community
in Christchurch, and around the country
all our migrants and refugees for whom Aotearoa New Zealand
was a place of safety and welcome—
all whose families and dreams were shattered, lives lost and
broken[1] by one hate-filled man who represents a voice our privilege
protects us from hearing—and the systemic racism at the heart of
"God's own country."

May we have the courage to speak up, speak out,
give nothing to racism: "no laughs, no likes, no attention, no power."
We give thanks for strong, compassionate and dynamic leadership,
especially as we are challenged to critique our own bias,
entitlement and complacency.

Wairua Tapu, Spirit of Earth and sea and sky
May we encourage our leaders in every decision,
every policy discussion, every change to legislation,
to actively engage with and honour Te Tiriti o Waitangi,
to use it as a framework for understanding,
for undoing the wrongs of colonialism
and restoring mana tangata whenua.
May the people of the land and the people of the Treaty together
show the world we *are* a place of mutual respect
and manaakitanga.

---

1 March 2019 Christchurch Mosques massacre

As the rabbi and healer Jesus taught us,
may we treat others as we would be treated.
May we never fall back into complacency.
Let us never again wander into the wilderness
of "not all kiwis" or "not all Pākehā" or "not all allies."
May we never again be the older brother
who's so busy being good
that we forget to plant the sunflower seeds
of forgiveness and compassion.
Transforming, transitioning Spirit, cloud by day and fire by night
May our rivers be ones besides which all peoples can
sing their songs, even in a strange land.

These are the words of our mouths and
the meditations of our hearts.

These are our prayers.

Blessing for Winter Meal

When winter seems darkest
and all is laid bare
the whole of creation is ours.

We gather for comfort, for courage, for change:
this abundance is ours to share.

We prune and shape, and let the new buds form.
We open our arms and turn our face to the light.
The fruit of our labours,
the bounty of earth is ours:
We share it and bless each other.

Prayers for Family

On the anniversary of law homosexual reform

O god who we create from the sum of all we know
that is wonderful, generous, just and wise
Creative spirit, Ground of our Being, Christ within:
Goddess and Gaia
Cosmic parent and Pentecostal flame
may we see ourselves in the god-ness of others
and ourselves in their image of you.

Oh god who changes through time
who appears in different guises,
in wind and fire, in storm and in stranger
whose names are numerous and whose voices are many
may we hear Sophia Wisdom in canticles and ballads,
workers' songs and lullabies
hear her sing in wilderness and marketplace.

When news headlines remind us of our vulnerable humanity,
of the violence so close beneath the skin
even in this beautiful land, we are aware
that there is still bullying and homophobia in our schools,
families torn by violence we call "domestic,"
prejudice against those we don't understand.

This month we celebrate the anniversary of Homosexual Law
Reform, yet still we must grieve for the lives of queer people of
colour killed in Orlando,[2] and for gay, lesbian, trans and bisexual
people who've died throughout the years,
and still die—at the hands of others or by suicide—
because although they wear your face,
their world does not welcome them.

We celebrate and honour the men, women and gender fluid people
who marched and petitioned and wore their rainbow colours
proudly, no matter the personal cost.

We honour those who still march, and vote, and sing
and who share their stories, in person and online.

On this anniversary of legislative change in Aotearoa
reform which recognised that love is love
regardless of gender or sexuality or orientation,
we celebrate our covenant to be an inclusive community.
May all know we are Christians by our love.

2   On 12 June 2016, a 29-year-old security guard killed 49 people and wounded 53 others in
    a mass shooting inside Pulse, a gay nightclub in Orlando, Florida

Oh god who manifests in rainbow ways,
as ancient wisdom and holy fool
as genderqueer, ungendered, cis and bi, straight and diverse
as prophet, story-spinner, jester and sage

be in the songs we sing
the wine we pour
the food we share.

Raindrops pizzicato

We give thanks for the rainy days as well as the sunny ones;
for leaves skipping and tumbling along the pavement;
for the pizzicato of raindrops on the roof,
and the smell of pine wood in an open fire.

We give thanks for the surprises life brings
just when we thought all possibilities had been exhausted,
and the ways that open,
when we thought all paths had been explored.

We give thanks for the wisdom that emerges
when we see the familiar from a new angle,
hear different memories of the same event,
or different meanings in remembered stories—
when we listen with new ears and open hearts.

Prayers on Father's Day

We give thanks for the carers who show us
that the truly strong are also kind.
For fathers and father figures who show
that caring is a strength, and tenderness can be powerful.

We hold in our hearts those working several jobs
to scrape together enough to live on and care for their families;

those whose learning difficulties or emotional impairment
weren't recognised soon enough to keep them from poor choices:
whose antisocial behaviour escalates into crime
and ends in psychiatric illness or prison.

We hold in our hearts those who've achieved a hard-won sobriety
or freedom from addiction—and those who've slipped off the wagon
when they were doing well, and now feel shame;

those who've lost their temper again when they've promised not to;
who've inflicted or been on the receiving end of family violence
and intimidation;

those who've never learned other ways to be family, to be strong.

May those of us blessed with secure upbringings and functional
families acknowledge how fortunate we are.

May we have greater empathy with men whose fragile egos
and low self-confidence are challenged and enraged
when social media go on about toxic masculinity and
criticize behaviours they've been raised to regard as normal.

May our efforts to educate and change behaviour
be inspired by respect and love for our fellow humans,
those we are tempted to call the least of our teacher
Jesus' brethren.

And may all children know the love of a strong and gentle figure,
formed in the image of Jesus' loving heavenly father,
who notices the fall of a sparrow,
and lovingly numbers the of hairs of their tousled, precious heads.

Spring in Aotearoa

September, October, November

Aotearoa Spring—prayers of pavement and city square

We give thanks for the tūī and bellbirds and baby sparrows
and the kōwhai and the freesias signalling spring
and offer praise by rushing out of doors to find a park
where we can walk barefoot on new-mown grass.

We go to the Gardens to worship the tulips
ride the hydraulic lift like angels
share a birdseed communion
with the ducks and ducklings
and laugh when blossom drops on someone's hair.

Or we make a pilgrimage to the countryside
rejoice in the lambs and calves
miraculous (to city folk) each year
and buy fresh eggs on the way home,
strawberries and nectarines.

The Aotearoa Spring
brings the seasonal winds
and grumbling we put on our jackets again.
The oak tree's vivid green, the rata's jaffa red,
the sea's like crinkled silver paper from an Easter egg
and we're grateful for the harbour breeze
as we walk uphill.

And about this time of year
the wise ones begin their star-led journey
while Joseph and Mary
are buying a donkey.

Pōhutukawa trees start to bud
and from pavement and mall and square
we give thanks for our city
in the spring.

We are blessed with enough

Prayers on World Communion Sunday

We give thanks that, in a world where starvation and obesity
affect billions, we are blessed with enough.

In a world where noise and sound and racket
can overwhelm us—city sounds: sirens, traffic,
crash of bins being emptied
wind rattling our windows.

Crowd sounds:
buskers, gossip, iPods, mobile conversations
isolating and connecting us.

In the clamour,
may we listen to each other's voices;
hear the still, small voice of calm.

In the many ways we are inspired:
silence and solitude for introverts
discussion and company for extroverts
through our eyes and ears, our hands and bodies
we experience the spirit.

With our words and actions, heads and hearts,
we listen and question, act and learn.

We share a common bread with the peoples of the world:
baguette or pita bread, naan, taco, bagel, couscous and rice.
We share a common cup with the peoples of the world:
wine, sake, lager; a pint at the pub with mates
cappuccino at our favourite café
sharing our troubles with a friend
Peace of Christ passed from hand to hand
in cups of tea and "bring a plate."

On World Communion Sunday
we give thanks that the table is open to all.
We take this hospitality on our journey;
this generosity into our world.

Botanical Gardens prayers

A traditional format for contemporary worship

Approach
We come to the Gardens to worship the tulips
share birdseed communion at the pond,
count blessings and ducklings.
Via the conifer way, a spell in the herb garden,
there's healing and refreshment
fragrance and cool green.

Confession
We're glad that we don't have to weed these edges
or drive the rubbish truck or clean the loos.
When we get home, forgive us
if we put food scraps down the insinkerator
because we can't make compost in the apartment,
or forget to plant a native tree when we fly long distance.

Petition and Intercession
The hothouse is full of people and begonias and ferns
the lily pads aren't big enough, yet, for frogs
and squealing kids try to catch the fish.

Remind us not to grumble when it's stuffy and humid
especially in overcoats against the breeze
or when people stop in front of us, cameras poised,
where we're trying to walk,
and the souvenirs are ridiculous prices.

Adoration and Praise
As the tulips die down, roses come into leaf;
there are shady paths to walk on,
poppies, delicate and strong,
and the year-round cottage garden.

Worldly-wise teenagers gather for picnics,
middle-aged lovers believe their luck at last,
there are blue and white irises
and opportune seats.

Absolution
We put our litter in the bin
and resolve to plant our own tomatoes next year,
and reduce our carbon emissions
by taking the bus or walking.

Thanksgiving
For the daffodils and jonquils, for magnolias and lilies
for colours, shapes and fragrance.
For our city's public gardens
and the Aotearoa springtime
we give thanks.

With the Spring comes the greening

Creative spirit, Ground of our Being, the Christ within:
In the lives of those around us, we see ourselves.
As we do unto others,
so are our actions, words and thoughts returned.
May our kindly impulses, generous wishes, thoughtful prayers
become the words that we speak and the things that we do.

Leader: With the spring comes the greening

Response: *From our passion come our actions.*

We give thanks for the goodness of rain
and the greatness of sunshine!
For regeneration in the cooler months, and the promise of spring.
We acknowledge the greening force,
in nature's vegetation and in us.
We give thanks for good health and think of those
whose lives are touched by dis-ease.
We hold in our hearts those who are unwell, or grieving, or in need.

With the spring comes the greening

From our passion come our actions.

As we journey forward together, may this truly be a place
where the desire for beauty and the care for others flourishes.
In kauri and icon, in bread and wine, in worship and shared meals,
we celebrate and build the commonwealth of freedom here,
in our community.

With the spring comes the greening;

From our passion come our actions.

September in Aotearoa brings not only the spring, but Father's Day.
We celebrate good parenting, whoever it's done by;
we hold in our hearts
those who haven't experienced the care of loving families;
and we give thanks for the caregivers of all sorts in our lives,
for those who help us become all we're meant to be,
and who remind us that we are loved.

As we receive, so may we pass on the light, the love.

Sometimes Spring

Sometimes spring comes
not in new leaf green and the frolic of lambs
but in the slime and leftovers of winter,
gutters of dank leaves,
and the colours of spring are jonquil pale,
grape hyacinth blue—
dark, deep blue and fragile.

Sometimes the golden daffodils signal cancer
and a spring wind slices the smile off our face.
We clutch the dark of winter
to our hearts, despair's familiar scarf up to our necks
and smell the decomposing dreams
of musty bulbs, not planted.

Yet we believe—
after the chill, the thaw
and azure skies, and blossom trees, and tulips' blaze will come
and slim tendrils of faith
will crack our densest walls, finding the sun

And spring is here, tight fronds unfurling
and summer will follow: Christ reborn in our land

So we give thanks
So we give thanks
So we give thanks.

Vigour of rain and passion of sunshine

We give thanks for the vigour of rain and the passion of sunshine,
for regeneration in cooler times, and the promises of spring.

In our gardens, the bulbs and blossoms
thrill us with their graceful miracles.

In our lives, small kindnesses and loving friends
encourage us in times of difficulty or stress,
and push the boat out with us in our times of joy.

In our world, those who work for peace
and the integrity of our planet
remind us that all life is precious.
So we give thanks.

Seasons in one day

Resources for the "ordinary" days

Reflections and essays

Allies or Traitors

A Reflection on Waitangi Day

On the night that felt like betrayal but was just over-enthusiastic "we know what's best" actions by well-meaning allies, Jesus gathered with his friends.

It was a closed group, confidants he could share ideas with and be his true self. His friends. Who loved him, admired him, who wore his t-shirt and marched under his banner—but who in the end, didn't honour the covenant relationship between them.

And yet, he understood them. He washed their feet and blessed them. He served the bread himself, and poured the wine, saying,

> "This is a new treaty between us. Share the bread and wine. Share my words, and my lifeblood, and my blessing. Share my bruises and victimisation, too; share the contempt of people who've never met me. Because when you do, you'll remember the promise: of tino rangatiratanga, the kingdom of heaven here, of bullying and oppression ended, of racism eradicated and the hungry fed. Share this life; walk in my shoes. Even if it's in your imagination, live my life."

"Wash all of me," cries Peter. "Not just my feet, but my hands and head and all of me. Of course, we'll never betray you."

"But have you really listened?" asks Jesus. "When I talk about the treaty and how to fulfil it, do you believe me? Or do you still want to do it your way, and feel hurt when you hear, 'That's not what we needed'?"

And then an argument broke out, over who'd been the best allies. They betrayed the Covenant between friends, because even if they heard him, they didn't *listen*. Sure, they agreed things weren't fair and needed to change. When it came to action, they wore the button, they had special t-shirts printed, they marched.

But if there was serious trouble, if people were going to get hurt, or there was looting or rioting instead of nice, peaceful palm-waving, they were out of there. If he chose to get among those sorts of people, and suffer, even risk getting killed, well, it wasn't really their fight, was it?

They'd signed online petitions and written letters and shared posts, but when someone muttered, "Nothing good ever came from

Nazareth—or Mangere, or Porirua," they edged away. And if the curious or confrontational said, "What's he really like? You know him, don't you?," they were like, "Not me. I agree with some of what he says, but he goes too far. Excuse me..." and off they slip, into the quieter crowds, away from the tired and disillusioned and angry ones.

Say her name.

Black Lives Matter.

I can't breathe.

Queer black lives matter.

Don't shoot me.

Say *their* names.

Black Lives Matter. It's a vibrant, grassroots movement in the United States that grew out of the unspeakable killings of black men, women, children, genderqueer folx, by state and government sanctioned police officers. Black people and people of colour gathering to say, "Enough! Don't kill us. We matter too."

And of course, the backlash. The people in authority's excuses. She should have done as she was told. He shouldn't have pulled a toy gun. She shouldn't have been answered back. He shouldn't have run. She wasn't innocent, that one. He was known to us. He looked like a troublemaker. Why was he wearing a hoodie? Why was she out so late at night? What was he doing driving a fancy car?

The backlash, the bullets, the brutality of power.

And then the crown of thorns. The "just saying" comments of the privileged. The ignorance. But we *didn't know*. We weren't taught it in school. I've never heard of Jim Crow. I'd never heard of Parihaka. No-one told me. Or, how come you've got this fancy job? Bet you got a race-based scholarship. Always wanting special treatment. Go back where you came from.

And if they answer, you mean Alabama, or New York City or Auckland, they're told not to be uppity. You can't be really human if half of you are in prison and the rest are unemployed or drug dealers or get pregnant to get a benefit. How dare you have five kids if you can't look after them? Why was your teenager out late anyway? What was he doing with a toy gun? Don't you know what's appropriate?

Or, how can you say I've got privilege? It's not my fault, no one cares if I lose my job, or the factories close. No one can say I shouldn't own as many guns as I want. Don't act like you're underprivileged when you've had a university education and I worked my way up from nothing.

The thorny crowns rammed on by the privileged.

And then, there's the betrayal by friends, the crucifixion by allies. The whining, and the fragility, and, "I'm doing my best. I wear my safety pin. A word of thanks would be good. You know, we're supporting you, we're standing with you, we don't have to. We're good people and do the right thing, so a bit of encouragement wouldn't hurt."

The expectation that others do the work.

"If we're not doing the right thing, why don't you tell us politely? What can we do? Do you expect us to get our hands dirty right along with you?"

And what that means is, we haven't been listening. We haven't tried to imagine your life, your history, your fear for your children. We haven't confronted our friends or colleagues or family members who make racist remarks or homophobic asides or sexist jokes.

You're tired and you're angry, and you thought the Constitution, the Covenant, the Treaty included you. But at the same time as you work nights and study to get qualifications and lead social justice initiatives and support your families and raise your kids and teach them fear as well as respect, really, haven't you got time to educate me? I admit I'm privileged, but can't you just spoon feed me a bit? I want to be an ally. I think I'm one. How come you're questioning my sincerity?

The betrayal by friends, the crucifixion by allies.

You know about the post-Brexit safety pins? Some people in the UK started wearing safety pins to show their stance against racism and their solidarity with immigrants—and tweeted photos of themselves wearing them. In the wake of the US election, the safety pin strategy caught on among white people there. And now they're feeling offended if a person of colour says, "If I'm being insulted or intimidated or attacked, I don't have time to look around and hope one of you well-meaning white people has a safety pin on their jacket." That it's feel-good tokenism and doesn't help.

So why does the "Black Lives Matter" movement mean so much, to me, here in Aotearoa New Zealand? To the tiny number of friends—Māori, queer, a few Pākehā—who acknowledge the articles I share, the hashtags and the heartfelt paragraphs begging white people to confront their privilege and listen to black people and people of colour?

Much of the information I've gathered about Black Lives Matter comes from my Black friend in Austin, Texas. One of the most gregarious, educated, independent women I've ever met tells me her mixed-race daughter is scared to go out much. And one of the Black teenagers police killed was a relative. And she's got the resources and the passion and the ability to spread the word—and she's *angry.*

And because I see and read and hear the parallels here. I'm frightened of the racism simmering under the covers of She'll Be Right, and It's a Good Place to Bring Up Kids, and We All Get Along, and We're better than the Aussies because we've got The Treaty. Because it's not like that.

I'm frightened, and I'm getting uncomfortable, and I want to do something! Because I still hear people start sentences with, "I'm sorry, but Māori are like that," and "I'm not racist, but...," or "Māoris can be racist, too," or "I knew him when his name was Steve."

So I asked in a Māori forum, would it be presumptuous of me to start an online group along the lines of *Māori Lives Matter to Pākehā, too*—and here's the reply: "The more people that can raise the issue of the big festering scab that lies beneath the surface of colonisation, which is intergenerational institutional racism, the better. Such a page would need someone behind it with broad shoulders and thick skin as you/the page would receive a lot of hate."

And I realise again how privileged I am that I can make the choice, that I can avoid all the aggro, while tangata whenua cannot.

In one of his last songs before he died, Leonard Cohen wrote the heart-rending,

> "I wish there was a treaty we could sign...
> I'm angry and I'm tired all the time.
> I wish there was a treaty, between your love and mine."

As a Canadian Jew who took Jesus Christ seriously, at the end, Cohen chose to be laid to rest in a traditional Jewish rite in a family plot. And when I listen to *Treaty*, I hear his disillusionment with the Christianity he's explored, although not with the "beautiful guy, Jesus" he once described.

I think of the Covenant between God and Abraham, the Covenant represented to Noah by a rainbow, the Covenant between Jesus and his friends on the night they were to betray him. And I think about Waitangi Day, and the Covenant this country, Aotearoa, has between its peoples. I hear Eddie Durie say that "Pākehā are the Tangata Tiriti, those who belong to the land by right of that Treaty."

I think of my Black friend in Austin, Texas, who's tired and angry at having to keep explaining to White people—including her friends—about how to be a true ally, and about white privilege, and white fragility and defensiveness. Suggesting that instead of asking her, they should be educating themselves and figuring out what to be and do. She's tired and she's angry, but she keeps sharing and posting and marching and preaching and educating.

And understanding that, "When we know better, we do better."

"Won't go away, Treaty won't go away.
Treaty, written in the skies.
Treaty, written in the hearts of mankind."

Moana and the Moa Hunters, Rua (1998).

Are my shoulders wide enough? Could my White fragility cope with the hate? Is my White skin thick enough? I'd need allies: and we'd get the disdain and the thorns and be metaphorically crucified for speaking out. But will you join me, anyway?

This Waitangi weekend, this Century, let us evolve God's Kindom of self-determination for all, where Treaty and Covenant are honoured. Not just in this whare karakia, but throughout this land, so all are respected and restored to dignity, rangatiratanga.

Maybe we should wear *our* safety pins on the inside, by our hearts—as a constant reminder: open, so the micro-aggressions, the pinpricks are real to us, too.

Tātou tātou e. Amen.

Blessed be the work of our hands

A Labour Weekend Reflection

"True religion is real living;
living with all one's soul,
with all one's goodness and righteousness."

Albert Einstein

Establish the work of our hands, prayed Moses in Psalm 90.

"May the favour of the Lord our God rest upon us; establish the work of our hands for us." That's in the New International Version. Another translation says, "Let the beauty—or sum of His gracious acts, in their harmony—be illustrated in us, and favour our enterprise."

What might it mean, for the beauty of God to be illustrated in us, and establish the work of our hands?

I wasn't happy with many of the commentaries about this text. Overall, they seemed to imply that, really, human work is shoddy. Most assumed an interventionist God, an external Source of beauty or favour that—if we work hard or believe very hard, or if we're lucky—might reflect well on us and what we do.

For this Labour Sunday, there were other themes I could have developed for this reflection. And yet, these words stuck in my mind, *"Establish the work of our hands."*

What might we make of them?

So, here's Moses, not even allowed into the Promised Land—when reaching it has been his life's work. Think of all he's been through:

The miraculous rescue from the Nile by the Pharaoh's daughter, and being raised in the palace.

Escaping into the desert after murdering an Egyptian slave master.

Hearing the Word coming from a burning bush: "Pick up your rod, Moses. Use your power—speak to Pharaoh!"

His struggle with a speech impediment, calling on his brother Aaron for help—but finally getting the words out: "Let my people go!"

The triumphant dance with Miriam and Aaron on crossing the Red Sea.

Then wandering through the wilderness for decades, with those undisciplined ex-slaves now wanting to go their own way, wanting golden idols and fatted calves and quail and sweetmeats instead of manna, wanting wine and roses instead of water from the rock.

After all this, where does Moses end up?

A hundred and twenty years old, buried in Moab, no-one knows where his grave is—and Joshua got to cross the River Jordan and trumpet Israel's victorious invasion of Jericho!

There's a Rabbinical tradition about these final verses of Psalm 90: that they were the original prayer that Moses recited as a blessing on the work of making the Tabernacle and its ornaments, and that afterwards he used them as the formula of benediction for any newly undertaken task, whenever God's Glorious Majesty was to be consulted for an answer by Urim and Thummim—the stones on the high priest's breastplate.

Sometime in there—between sorting out inter-tribal rivalries, and making sure only the purest lambs were used for sacrifices, facing his family's disapproval of his mixed-race marriage, completing the Tabernacle in the wilderness, with all its ornaments, keeping an eye out for that pillar of cloud by day and fire by night—Moses has time and energy to sit down and write, or perhaps, stand up and pray:

> "For a thousand years in thy sight are but as yesterday when it is past, and as a watch in the night... Let thy work appear unto thy servants, and thy glory unto their children. And let the beauty of the LORD our God be upon us: and establish thou the work of our hands upon us; yea, the work of our hands, establish thou it."

Perhaps Moses truly appreciated and understood his life's work. Perhaps he took a long-term view—a hundred years or a thousand are like a day gone by, or like the night watch; it seems long, but how quickly it is done.

With the succession planning taken care of, he may have been happy to lie down at the end of the very long day, and let Joshua take over. Maybe Moses knew how well established the work of his hands was and didn't need to see it through to the very end.

And what did Jesus have to say? When questioned by legal experts about the law—and much of the law involved what work you could and couldn't do, who you could and couldn't work with, and when, how particular tasks were to be done down to the last detail—Jesus responded:

> "Love the Lord your God with all your heart and with all your soul and with all your mind. This is the first and greatest commandment. And the second is like it: Love your neighbour as yourself."

Sounds relatively simple, doesn't it?

Provided, of course, you've learned to love yourself, to love that of *you* which is God, to see and love the God in your neighbours.

Even the noisy ones, the messy ones, the ones who play their music too loud or mow their lawns too early in the morning.

The neighbours who paint their homes in ghastly colours or have mates around who, really, aren't quite who you'd expect in your neighbourhood, with their rusty cars and their tinnies and their bizarre language.

Or who wait at the bus stop, mumbling and dribbling, or take your seat when your feet are tired and you've got umpteen shopping bags.

Or whose inner beauty didn't get much chance to shine, from years of neglect as children or domestic abuse as adults.

Or the neighbours who whine a lot: the incessant writers-to-the-editor, the ones we wish would get a life, the doom-sayers and gloom merchants, the office whingers, the ones who try to take the shine off others' achievements.

Those neighbours.

Love *them* with all our hearts and with all our souls and with all our minds—that's one way to establish the work of our hands. Or maybe, we should get on with loving through our actions first, in faith that our hearts will catch up.

While thinking about this service I was reading Tim Farrington's novel, *The Monk Downstairs*. A man leaves a life of contemplation after some 20 years in the monastery and confronts what "real work" might be. He gets a job at McDonalds, and forms a relationship with the single mother whose basement he rents, and with her daughter, who he helps care for when his new friend's mother has a stroke.

Some of the plot's predictable but what made the story unusual is that it's interspersed with letters this former monk writes to a friend and sparring partner who's still in the monastery—quoting Thomas Merton and Brother Lawrence, John of the Cross and the prophet Jeremiah.

In these letters he explores his changing feelings about the lives of contemplation and of paid work, of the effort that goes into relationships, and his discovery that "the life fulfilled in love" isn't lounging in a soft chair, that "we do not serve that larger Love" by giving up on the grittiness of life, of human love.

"We are born to love as we are born to die, and between the heartbeats of those two great mysteries lies all the tangled growth of our tiny lives," he discovers—the tangle of priorities and commitments and energy and sacrifice involved in loving our neighbour.

While he realises that, his busy new friend and lover finds unexpected meaning in the quiet times, the contemplation and silence and enforced "Sabbath rest" of sitting with her mother, by a hospital bed, for long hours. In a way, they're changing places, like Martha and Mary. The value of work, of occupation, the value of listening and contemplation—which is the better part?

Or, as the lawyers asked Jesus, "Which is the greatest commandment?"

The character in the novel finds, with John of the Cross, that we must go forth and behold ourselves in divine beauty:

> To the mountain and to the hill,
> To where the pure water flows,
> And further, deep into the thicket.

Not either/or, not acting or listening, not rushing or resting, but both/ all.

In *Thoughts for the Inner Life,* Jessie Coombs commented on Psalm 90. The language assumes an external, all-powerful and interventionist deity, but her response is one we can hear with 21st century ears.

In 1867, Coombs wrote:

> "Our work and Divine Beauty, at first sight, how different; yet, on deeper insight, how truly one, how inseparably united. There is light so beauty-giving, that nothing it touches is positively ugly... Who of us has not marvelled at an unexpected light, in what we had always thought an uninteresting face? Who has not beheld a light divine irradiate the human countenance, giving joy, and prophesying perfection, where we had least thought to find beauty?...

> You know what the natural light can do for material objects; you know what mental and moral light can work for human faces; rise from these, and know what spiritual light, Divine Light, can do for immortal beings and immortal works."

There's the God-beauty in us, when we see "a light divine" irradiate another human countenance, where we had not expected to see beauty. The way goes not just past the still waters, but through the valley of shadows, into the deep thicket.

In *Universe Is a Green Dragon*, Brian Swimme writes:

> "This is the only time you have to show yourself. You can't hold back or hide in a cave. You can't waste away in a meaningless job, cramming your life with trivia... What we bestow on the world allows others to live in joy... We ignite life in others... We become beauty to ignite the beauty of others... We work to enchant others, to ignite life, to enhance the unfolding of being..."

And in *Tomorrow's God,* Lloyd Geering reminds us that,

> "The meaning of human existence will increasingly become one of caring for the earth... caring for all life on earth and caring for one another...
>
> This imperative to take care must take precedence over lesser loyalties and over all differences of race, nationality, gender and personal beliefs. It is the kind of love which is ready to sacrifice self-interest for the greater good of the whole. We shall be required to limit our own early pleasures and expectations in the interests of generations yet to be born.
>
> Like Moses of old on Mount Nebo looking to the Promised Land, we need to show our concern for a future world that we ourselves shall never enter. This calls for the kind of self-sacrificing love which has long been affirmed in the Christian tradition and symbolised as the way of the cross."

These are the great commandments for our time: "Love the earth and all that it contains; Love your neighbour—as you love yourself—with everything that's in you."

As Moses knew and Jesus taught, and as Albert Einstein wrote, "True religion is real living; living with all one's soul, with all one's goodness and righteousness."

Thus the work of our hands is established—recognised, justified—when we work "to enhance the unfolding of being..." In these ways, our enterprise is favoured, and the divine beauty shines in us.

Blessed be the work of our hands.

Feast in the wilderness (i): Next year in Jerusalem

Imagine you're sitting around a table.

The best tablecloth, the best china's on the table. There are flowers and candles. It's the end of winter, the beginning of spring. The sun has set, a very busy day is over. It is Friday night.

Now, in imagination, step back a little, to earlier in the day. Whatever your occupation, you've been working hard—in paid or unpaid employment, studying, cleaning the house, cooking...

Out there in the world, perhaps you don't fit in. Think of a time you were made to feel odd or unwanted or unworthy. Perhaps because of what you believe, how you look, how you behave—who you are. In some way, for whatever reason, imagine life for you is unsafe. Your family may be stigmatised or threatened, your lifestyle unwelcome in what was your community. Perhaps this is your experience, or memories from your parents' or grandparents' lives.

And now, light the candles! Here you are again, around the table with family and friends, in relative safety, among your own people.

There is food—plain food: unleavened bread, lettuce and herbs, roast lamb, fruit sauce, a roasted egg. There are dishes containing saltwater for dipping, glasses of wine, wine and water for the children. The leader may be wearing a white robe, perhaps he or she sits on a pillow. Breaking in half three pieces of unleavened bread the leader sets one half aside, and holding up the remaining pieces, says, "This is the poor bread that our ancestors ate in Egypt..."

Now the youngest child asks, "Why is this night different from all other nights?" and the leader tells the story of Exodus and Passover.

The meal, the liturgy, continues. Wine is drunk, food eaten, the door opened to imaginatively greet Elijah the Prophet. Everyone praises God and sings closing songs. And the leader ends the liturgy, saying, "Next year in Jerusalem!"

Feast in the wilderness (ii): The Promised Land

Imagine you're at a table...

You may be in company or alone. Recall the comfort of shaking off dust and bathing your feet, refreshing your wrists in cool water.

You might perch on a camp stool or lounge on soft cushions. You could feast on manna from heaven or still be gnawing on the poor bread of your ancestors.

Does water gush from the rock, or do you still hunger and thirst for righteousness? Is your throat too dry to croak out the Lord's song in a strange land, or do you sing and dance on the far shore of the River Jordan? Are you a light on the way, leaven in the bread?

The sun is setting at the end of a busy day.

For now, you are safe. There are flowers on the table—exotic blooms or wildflowers from the path. It may be a night like other nights or a rare, Sabbath rest.

Drink the water or wine. Smell the everyday, mysterious bread, symbol of liberation and test. Eat it, all.

Consider the year ahead. Are you nearing journey's end?

Do you recognise the Promised Land?

Loving Boldly—What makes a leader?

First Testament prophets were a "diverse range of individuals." Some 500 years of prophetic activity is recorded in the Hebrew scriptures, in a changing political context which included Israel's pre- and post-Exile experience.

What might we learn from them about who is fit to lead and minister in our church? Who is called to the prophetic vision?

Theologian and retired Bishop John Shelby Spong describes the first testament prophets as "intensely human," moreover, he concludes, prophets spoke to and for their times, "to remedy the intensely human problems of injustice and the loss of meaning," and—as in the case of Isaiah—help their people deal with the trauma of exile. Lloyd Geering describes prophets—along with seers, philosophers and artists—as asking basic questions about meaning.

Think now on the apparent behaviour of the prophets—those called by God to share God's word to God's people.

Prophets, it seems, did not just preach visionary sermons: many of them violated good taste, they broke pots (Jeremiah), married whores (Hosea) and walked around naked (Isaiah). This behaviour has been dignified with the title, "performative prophecy." No wonder Martin Luther thought the prophets unedifying! Not only did they rail against the social conditions of their day, but they also behaved in socially embarrassing ways.

Moses stutters to a "burning bush" and Elijah stages the Mt Carmel contest with the Prophets of Baal, mocking and taunting them to a frenzy, and on "winning," has them slaughtered. Not only that, he disappears into the sky in a blaze of chariot wheels, leaving his cloak to poor Elisha who must have regretted signing up for prophet school. Ezekiel's imagination is indescribable, and Saul goes barking mad.

Little wonder, perhaps, that some hearers hardened their hearts against the prophets and treating them as "a laughingstock."

But—did God vote that these people weren't fit to be leaders?

Poor Jonah tried desperately to escape, and God pursued him even to the belly of a fish. Nahum, with no qualms about running for days by the King's chariot and then accusing him of forgetting the way of the Lord, might have stopped to think about the nature of his personal relationships. So might Abraham, instead of dragging Isaac, the miraculous son of his old age, up a mountain, apparently intent on ritually slaughtering him. What sort of prophetic vision is worth the life of your only child? What sort of family relationship does that represent?

Let's look at a prophet's personal profile: first testament prophets had most of these characteristics or experiences in common:

- A call narrative—a sense of vocation, of being called by God
- A sense of reluctance, but having no choice but to accept "the call"
- Vision: "a mode of seeing" and a reformative message
- Unsympathetic listeners, for the most part
- Manifesting their message in their personal life
- Experience of grief: characterised by "suffering servant," the "man of sorrow"
- Connection with the state, cities, urban life and politics
- A "burning force": prophets often felt they must proclaim a message that they hated, criticize the nation and chastise the people they loved.

Does anything in that list sound familiar?

In questioning the power structures of their day, many prophets were truly subversive, their messages and actions were effective, if unpopular, ways of gaining attention. As Bishop Desmond Tutu observed, the bible is indeed the most subversive book.

The passion of the prophets was to restore righteousness and justice in their nation and their peoples—their faith community— where high and low would be equal before God.

A burning message of righteousness
So what is this "burning message of righteousness" that some people will listen to, respond to, act on? The recurring themes of the prophetic message were, (a) the righteousness of God— often considering how the king, state or nation would be if they demonstrated God-like integrity, promise-keeping and justice, and (b) social justice—prophets highlighted the gap between the suffering of their people and what their experience would be in a just nation. (We might add, in a just denomination or church community.)

The compilers of the prophetic books have them conclude poignantly in many instances, with the prophets still despairing after a lifetime of work. Yet each contains a vision of hope:

Jeremiah concludes:

> "They will be my people, and I will be their God, for they will return to me with all their heart."

Zechariah:

> "Shout and be glad, O daughter of Zion... Many nations will be joined with the Lord... and will become my people."

Micah:

> "In the last days the mountain of the Lord's temple will be established... He will teach us his ways, so that we may walk in his paths... He will judge between many peoples and will settle disputes for strong nations far and wide. They will beat their swords into ploughshares and their spears into pruning hooks. Nation will not take up against nation, nor will they train for war anymore. Every[one] will sit under [their] own vine and under [their] own fig tree, and no one will make them afraid..."

Validity of a call

A passionate vision of social justice and equality will be needed as far into the future as power is unfairly shared between peoples and the planet's resources are over-exploited. We must resist false prophets who seek to twist the Word of God and, as Martin Buber writes, "sew it into their quilt of motley illusions."

In our day, who are fit speakers for an immanent God, a God who permanently pervades the universe, including human persons?

"A prophet's personal certainty of a call," writes James Ward in *The Context of the Prophetic Message*, "was not sufficient grounds for the community's acceptance of a prophet's word as the word of God." The way to tell an authentic prophet from a false one was two-fold: if the prophet said to worship other gods, you must not heed them, for probably God is testing you, but if God's word came to pass, the prophet was a true one.

What if our self-judged "acceptable" leaders say it's not just okay but necessary to discriminate against others on grounds that violate basic human rights? To worship the gods of literalism, judgement, prejudice rather than of justice, inclusivity, love?

In the past, the word of God appeared to come via prophets, and no doubt their authenticity took time to prove (especially as God sometimes put false words in their mouths to test their hearers' discernment). Increasingly in our day, the word of God comes more directly and via a range of media. Our prophets may be philosophers and artists, storytellers and scientists, public servants and songwriters.

Karen Armstrong suggests that, for those repelled by the idea of a personal God, the God of the Mystics might be an acceptable substitute:

> "This God is to be approached through the imagination and can be seen as a kind of art form, akin to the other great artistic symbols that have expressed the ineffable mystery, beauty and value of life... Like all art, however, mysticism requires intelligence, discipline and self-criticism as a safeguard against indulgent emotionalism and projection."

Can there be authentic prophecy without authentic hearers?

For an authentic message to emerge, the prophetic message needs "authentic" hearers: an audience prepared to use its discernment, to judge if the prophecy is fitting—whether it constitutes the word of God for its time. In listening to each other, we learn to understand ourselves, our God-selves, and to hear the voices of the imagination, see the visions of righteousness.

In our day, not only those with the job title of prophet or minister have a responsibility to share the Word of God for our time. In creating a just future, we must all be prophets and seers, speakers and singers, creators of symbols and dreams. We all have a role in highlighting the gap between a just civilization and the suffering of earth and its peoples.

In creating the future, we must all—gay, straight, bi, transgender, coupled or single, alone and in community—become both prophet and prophecy: manifesting the integrity of God and the delivering the earth from bondage.

How are we going to do this? Where do we find the courage to share our burning message of righteousness?

To begin with, in the very structures, in the relationships that some would seek to undermine: in loving relationships, in families of choice and of the heart, in learning through the love of another to love ourselves, for so the cup of loving multiplies.

So then do love and justice extend beyond our intimate circle to the communities and worlds in which we live. There we will find the courage, the energy, the faith—to ask basic questions about meaning, to remedy the problems of injustice, to violate good taste—behave in socially embarrassing ways—appear on television—sing songs of 'welcome home' at airports, to remind each other of the ineffable mystery, beauty and value of life.

Then, to quote both songwriter Pat Humphries and former Bishop Jack Spong, we'll find the courage, the energy, the faith to keep on "Loving Boldly"!

To work for change together. Never turning back.

Milk from the breast of Christ

Extract from Essay for Religious Studies course at Victoria University of Wellington, January 2000: "Is demythologization helpful in understanding the miracles of the Bible?"

Participating in or imaginatively entering the worldview of the storytellers—rather than utterly abandoning the three-tier world of the Bible narrators—can be effective in understanding miracles.

It's not necessary—although it can be useful—to strip the miracle stories of their magic and regard them from a scientific world view, so long as we provide an alternative the audience can respond to.

Whatever the method, it needs to be appropriate to the audience's purpose in wishing to understand and respond to the miracle.

I stand with friends and strangers in a circle around the communion table, palms upward to receive the bread and wine.

The late Professor Judith Dale has spoken movingly about Hildegard of Bingham and Julian of Norwich, including Julian's concept of Jesus as Mother.

Elders move around the circle with the loaf of bread and chalice of wine, murmuring, "The body of Christ for you," "Wine of the new covenant for you" to each communicant.

It is my turn to receive the wine. Rosemary looks me in the eye as she offers me the cup, and says, "Milk from the breast of Christ for you, Bronwyn." I suppress the urge to giggle; in context, her words are liturgical and appropriate and draw on our shared appreciation of the day's sermon.

Recalling this incident a couple of years later, I am surprised by my response: for years I have cheerfully if solemnly drunk "the blood of Christ" as part of the communion ritual, yet the idea of drinking "milk from the breast of Christ" makes me want to gag.

If I believed the bread and wine to be the actual body of Christ, if I was starving in the desert, would I prefer to drink blood or breast milk?

And when I allow myself to imaginatively enter a worldview where the Christ is a mother figure, the milk from Christ's breast as a symbol of spiritual sustenance becomes attractive. Recalling my own long-ago time as a breast-feeding mother, the experience of re-creation becomes at once more "real" and more "miraculous."

Put on your glad rags and break the rules!

What does it mean to leave one's gods and to choose a new god?

"Look, your sister-in-law has gone back to her people and her gods; return to them with her," says Naomi.

Ruth replies:

> "Don't beg me to leave you, or to return home instead of coming with you. For where you go, I will go, and where you live, I will live. Your community will be my community, and your god will be my god. Where you die, I will die, and be buried there."

For the participants of this story, God, land and people are one. Ruth uses an ancient oath formula. By saying when she dies, she will be buried in Naomi's land, she is emphasising her desire to identify with Naomi's people, her reality and community.[3]

At that time,

> "there was as yet no formal procedure for religious conversion, nor was it even conceived of. One's ethnic identity determined for all time one's religious persuasion. Therefore, Ruth mentions 'people' and 'God' together. Each people had its own god; or as it was viewed in the ancient Near East, each god had its own people. Ruth is adopting a new people, a new ethnic identity, along with a new faith."[4]

While Orpah her sister-in-law does what is proper and conventional, Ruth—and later, Boaz—go beyond convention and recognise no limits.

Here's a woman breaking with her traditions, breaking the rules of her culture and upbringing, to choose a new life in a strange land. She acts out of loyalty and love, which lead her on a barrier-breaking journey.

The story of Ruth operates on many levels, and we'll return to it in more detail. In contrast, the New Testament story of the widow at the synagogue seems slim. What do the stories of Ruth and "the widow's offering" have in common? If we can find no answers, what questions do they make us ask?

In the earlier story, there are three childless widows; in the New Testament story, we might speculate that the widow was also childless, as she appears to have no family to support her.

---

3   The Interpreter's Bible, p 837
4   The Harper Collins Study Bible, pp 410, 411

There's an expectation in both stories that those who are well off will provide for those who are poor. Over 400 years before the time of Jesus, as a widow and resident alien, Ruth was entitled to glean where she chose. We could assume that the systems of caring for the poor were even more highly developed by Jesus' day; certainly the Jews seem hemmed about with laws and rituals which Jesus constantly challenged. "...Widows were traditionally considered subjects of special moral concern because of their generally defenceless legal and financial position."

In each story, wealthy, land-owning, learned men appear: Ruth is taken as wife by one of the great men of the city, and the marriage is formally approved by all those in authority and by the people at large; the scribes, or learned men, walk around in long robes and like be greeted with respect in the marketplace and to have the best seats at the banquet. Boaz is described as "a great man," and we find no *criticism* of the flowing robes—their glad rags: Jesus doesn't condemn them for wanting to be acknowledged or trying to get the best seats at the festival! Rather, he criticises them, among other things, for "... appointing some supposedly reputable and pious man to oversee the affairs of a widow, only to use the estate for his gain."[5]

In each instance, the customs and rulings which govern people's lives are questioned.

Whatever was meant by Mark's telling the story and Jesus' comments on the widow who gave all she had, we can compare her offering with Ruth's. The widow "put in more than all those who are contributing to the treasury. For all of them... contributed out of their abundance, but she out of her poverty has put in everything she had, all she had to live on"—literally, says Jesus, "her whole life."[6]

And what did Ruth have to give? Travelling with Naomi from Moab to Israel, from the land of emptiness to the land of plenty, Ruth apparently has nothing to give—except her loyalty and love. In seeking Boaz's protection and the redemption of Naomi's land, Ruth gives all that she has—her body, her potential as the bearer of a child, her future: we might say, her whole life.

For shortly after this, Ruth drops out of her own story. Having presented her mother-in-law with a son, she is not mentioned again. Naomi nurses the child, the local women name him, and they even proclaim, 'A son has been born to Naomi'... Ruth, the ostensible heroine of the story, is left an enigma. Remember this for later!

---

5   The Women's Bible Commentary, p 270
6   The Harper Collins Study Bible, p 1943

Likewise, it seems Jesus objectifies the widow at the treasury, referring to a woman with whom he apparently never interacts, as an example of the exploiting power structures of the time.

As Jesus watches from the sidelines, perhaps although he can do nothing for her at the moment, she does something for him. The *Women's Bible Commentary* suggests,

> "Her presence may lead Jesus to accept his final collision with the power that determines his fate. [In giving her whole life] She inspires Jesus to be truly Jesus... From her behaviour which can objectively be said to be meaningless, and from Jesus' reaction to it, we can only acknowledge the inclusive scope of the community of faith Jesus proclaims..."[7]

Can the poor widow whose reward is unknown, and Ruth who finds a new life in a new community, inspire us to be truly ourselves?

Now, let's return to Bethlehem. In the journey of Ruth from Moab, in the promise of a son, can we see the kernel of a later journey tale?

The story of Ruth is carefully structured, and there are hints of an older tale recounted, a folk story retold—details added and discarded—to suit the teller's purpose and the life and times of the listeners.

One commentary suggests that

> "Certain details in the book of Ruth may once have adorned a tale of the Babylonian Ishtar, to whom Esther owes her name... It is even possible that the outline of the story of Naomi, the 'pleasant one', who after her lament for her sorrows is comforted by the child who takes the place of the dead, comes from a myth once told or recited in liturgy by the priests of the fertility cult which gave Bethlehem its name. There, even in Jerome's day, stood a grove of Adonis."[8]

What is the significance of this story? For it's not *just* a perfectly formed tale, balancing Orpah against Ruth, the unnamed kinsman against Boaz, prolonging suspense while we wait to see if the kinsman will marry Ruth, his handing over of the sandal to indicate that he is giving up his claim.

The most significant thing about Ruth is her foreignness. "She seeks and finds refuge 'under the wings' of the God of Israel, she marries one of the great men of the city, the marriage is formally approved by all those in authority and by the people at large. The child of the marriage is adopted by Naomi, and that child's grandson is David the king."

---

7   Ibid
8   The Interpreter's Bible, p 830

A genealogy added to the book makes the connection between Naomi and Boaz and Ruth's child, tracing the family tree from Obed, to Jesse, to David—a family tree to whose branches a later storyteller added the ultimate birth story: Jesus, born in Bethlehem, to another unconventional young woman, a stranger to the town— Jesus, the ultimate rule-breaker.

The story reflects a truth which is implied in the Genesis genealogies, a truth which Jesus persisted in demonstrating, a truth that Peter reluctantly accepted and Paul proclaimed: that "God is no respecter of persons, but in every nation those that honour God are acceptable," that "in the Christ there can be neither Jew nor Greek, slave nor free, male nor female"—neither Hebrew nor Moabitess, landowner nor stranger, influential people making decisions at the gate nor foreigners seeking refuge.[9]

Have we, too, journeyed to a chosen Bethlehem, a place of promise, a place of scandal? Does the inclusiveness we claim, the social justice we espouse, the "place with no labels" by which we label this community, make this a land of transformation?

And who is Ruth, this childless widow? This scheming, seducing, law-breaking, ruthless Ruth—who loves so totally, offers such loyalty, that she finds in the fertile land of Bethlehem, a good harvest, family, security and a child of promise.

For Ruth is not just a loving daughter-in-law, a loyal family member, a conventional wife. Her meeting with Boaz reverses the typical meeting stories found elsewhere in the bible, between couples who will eventually marry. Ruth takes on a man's role, leaving home to seek her fortune; she encounters hardships, she has water drawn for her.

This is a wily tale, full of euphemism and seduction.

At Naomi's suggestion, Ruth goes to gather grain; fortuitously, she finds herself on the property of Boaz, who—good landowner that he is—blesses the reapers and is blessed in return, and during this meeting of management and employees, he notices Ruth and asks who she is. The overseer explains that, "She is the Moabite who came back with Naomi." At this point, she is no one's wife, betrothed or servant, nor is she yet a member of the community.[10]

As a widow and resident alien, Ruth is entitled to glean where she chooses, but she requests Boaz's permission, and he makes sure she gathers the best grain, is not bothered by the men, is given water to drink, and invites her to share the communal meal. He

9 Ibid, p 831, 846
10 The Women's Bible Commentary

hands her food—as a spouse would do, when she's finished eating, she has food to spare, which she saves for Naomi.

Boaz arranges for his reapers to provide Ruth with extra grain, and Naomi is astounded by Ruth's good fortune and offers a blessing to the one who took notice of Ruth. Naomi may be offering a prayer to her god, but Ruth insists that the one who caused her good fortune was Boaz. She twists Boaz's words, telling Naomi he'd suggested she keep close to his young men, when in fact he'd told her to keep close to the women.

Naomi advises Ruth to glean among the women. She recalls that Boaz is a male relative, who may act as a redeemer, saving family members from slavery and exile, and ensuring property remains in the family.

"Put your glad rags on," says Naomi! "Get dressed up," she tells Ruth, "Wash and put on perfume and go down to the threshing floor." There, Ruth is to find where Boaz lies down, in a contented mood after eating and drinking, and "uncover his feet"—Naomi politely uses a euphemism for genitals. Boaz, Naomi says, will tell Ruth what to do.

The threshing floor, not so incidentally, is associated with sexual activity, probably related to celebrations of the spring harvest. After all, this is Bethlehem, shrine of a fertility cult, and this year there's a splendid harvest!

At midnight, Boaz wakes, disturbed, and realises this woman is next to him. Earlier in the fields, he recognised Ruth as the loyal and loving daughter-in-law of Naomi; he's commended her for not going after younger men, ensured the men do not shame or molest her; he has acknowledged her as a woman of worth, and prayed that her full reward will come from the deity under whose wings Ruth has come for refuge. The word for wings is the same as that for cloak; it, too, can suggest genitalia.

Ruth now repeats Boaz's earlier words, asking him to "spread his cloak over her and redeem her"—a request full of implications. Contrary to Naomi's suggestion, *Ruth* tells *Boaz* what to do. And where Boaz had asked God to bless Ruth, she requests a blessing directly from Boaz—which he gives. He blesses her for accompanying Naomi and attempting to find a redeemer for them, and he asks her to stay the night.

But before dawn he sends her away, with a large quantity of barley. Perhaps he wishes to preserve Ruth's reputation or wants their relationship to be unknown to the next of kin, wants his motives to seem dispassionate and pious rather than personal and sexual.

No longer perceived as a foreigner, a servant, a handmaid or a daughter, Ruth is suitable for the role of Boaz's wife; Boaz has agreed to be her redeemer and protector, securing her future and protecting Naomi's land. So Ruth returns to her mother-in-law, and Naomi asks, "How did things go with you?" Ruth responds by pointing to the gift of barley and adds that Boaz did not want her to return empty handed to her mother-in-law.

In fact, Boaz had said no such thing, but Ruth adapts his words to include Naomi, and in her reply, perhaps there's another double entendre: Ruth symbolically carries what Naomi most wants—Boaz's seed. By handing Naomi the grain, Ruth is anticipating handing the child Obed to her mother-in-law. Through Ruth's efforts, Naomi— the who has changed her name from "pleasant" to Mara, meaning bitterness because she has returned from Moab empty—will no longer be empty-handed.

Ruth has left home, risked attack in the fields, placed herself and Boaz in a compromising position, lied to her mother-in-law: the text may be implying she's done all a woman can do, that it's through deceit and trickery that women gain redemption. But the trickster has a respected place in biblical tradition, and we shouldn't assume that Ruth is being condemned for her actions. Certainly when the townspeople hear of the marriage, they bless Ruth and wish for her fertility that she may build up Boaz's house as Rachel and Leah (in another tale of seduction and trickery) had done for Jacob.

And then, we hear no more of her. Ruth, the heroine of the story, disappears, "her continuing relationship to Naomi, her feelings for her son and husband, and her sense of belonging in Israel are never addressed."[11] She's completed her quest, and she's no longer essential to the narrative. The action moves to the future, to the branch of Jesse, the house of David, the longed-for redeemer.

"Look, your sister-in-law has gone back to her people and her gods, return to them with her," says Naomi to Ruth.

And Ruth's response?

> "Entreat me not to leave thee or forsake thee. For whither thou goest, I will go, and where thou lodgest, I will lodge. Thy people will be my people, and thy god, my god."

What tricks do we play on ourselves, pretending others—not we— are the strangers? What does it mean to redeem and secure our future, and ensure that we are not left empty? Who in these stories represents our community?

---

11 The Women's Bible Commentary, pp 83-84

Who do you identify with?

Do you feel like Orpah: torn between the challenge of a strange country, the love of a family of choice, and the pull of the old gods and traditions of the past? Do you feel safer doing what is proper and conventional, instead of confronting what it means to live in the land of plenty?

Do you feel like the poor widow: giving and giving, until you have nothing left? Do you feel you must glean in the fields, take other's leavings, instead of boldly seeking the generosity of this chosen family, and receiving a harvest so great that you have enough to share?

Sometimes, are we Boaz:? Wealthy, land-owning, learned, worthy—like the scribes by the treasury—good people, loyal people, doing what's required of us, wanting to be respectable. Needing to have our lives turned around by some rule-breaking, seductive, loving trickster who wears the face of the Christ.

Are we like Obed: a child of promise—born of a poverty-stricken, foreign mother from a far-off land, and a rich father who's seduced by the claims of family and the promise of a son?

Or David: shepherd boy and king, lover and sinner, descendent of Israel and Moab, minstrel and giant slayer?

Perhaps we're Mara: the empty one who needs the generosity and loving kindness of others to find healing, who need companions to go with us to a place of plenty and fulfilment. But we can become Naomi, who challenges us to put our glad rags on and secure the community's future.

Or are we Ruth: choosing a new god, a new family, a community which lets us explore and discard?

Have we the courage to put on our glad rags, break with convention and find true fulfilment: the kingdom of god seeded and growing in us, bearing a rich harvest?

In this place, where the old gods no longer control our seasons and old explanations no longer satisfy, we are challenged to give our whole lives, to growing this community where we are free to be our real selves—and ask the questions to which we are the answer.

So may it be.

Sacred stones and sites—reflection and liturgy

(Note for service leader: To prepare for delivering this reflection, you need a few large and a lot of smallish stones—I collected stones from a local beach. At the front of the venue, create a cairn with the larger stones and a few small ones. Have a container of stones at the entrance, so as the people arrive, they can take a stone along with their service sheet. In your welcome, ask them to hold the stone in their hand until the liturgy which will be part of the Reflection.)

Rocks—stones—pebbles.

Cairns, monoliths, gems.

From stones marking burial sites to medicine wheels or, more correctly, sacred hoops—from the standing stones of Europe to the sacred Vedic stones from the Krishna-Gandaki River in Nepal—from the Egyptian pyramids to Stonehenge in England and Stonehenge Wairarapa—ancient people created sacred structures of rock, revered stones as talismans or shrines, and created myths, symbols and rituals with and around them.

Among Māori, heirlooms or weapons of great status, often made of pounamu, were seen as being tapu (sacred) and having great mana (status). Stones were used as talismans to represent and protect mauri—the vitality, or life force of living and inanimate things.

And the metaphorical concept of tatu pounamu—a greenstone door—symbolised a passageway between the territories of warring parties. Each party to the peace pact chose a hill to represent the greenstone door, which was closed to all who wanted to draw blood. The enduring nature of pounamu symbolised the permanence of the peace agreement.

First Nations people of North America made medicine wheels, by laying stones in a particular pattern on the ground. Most have a central cairn of stones, surrounded by an outer ring of stones, then "spokes," or lines of rocks, coming out the cairn. One of the older wheels has been dated to over 4,500 years old. Like Stonehenge, it had been built up by successive generations who would add new features to the circle.

A custom of the Jewish faith is to put pebbles on a grave. This shows that someone has visited the grave and may have developed from the custom of writing notes to the deceased and pushing them into crevices in the headstone, just as notes are pushed into the Western Wall in Jerusalem. When no crevice could be found, the note was weighted down with a stone. In time, the paper disintegrated or blew away leaving only the stone. Thus, some began to think that leaving a stone was the custom... and so it became the custom.

The rite of laying a cornerstone is an important cultural component of eastern architecture and metaphorically in sacred architecture generally. Often, the ceremony involved placing of offerings of grain, wine and oil on or under the stone: symbolic of the produce and the people of the land and the means of their subsistence. This in turn derived from the practice in still more ancient times of making an animal or human sacrifice that was laid in the foundations.

The cornerstone (or foundation stone) was the first stone set in the construction of a masonry foundation. All other stones were set in reference to this stone, determining the position of the entire structure.

Many of our Judeo-Christian stories involve sacred stones and rocks:

Jacob sleeping in the desert with a stone for a pillow. Moses' victory song: "The best of Pharaoh's officers is drowned in the Red Sea. The deep waters have covered them, they sank to the depths like a stone." Later, Moses on the mountain where God says, "There is a place near me where you may stand on a rock. I will put you in a cleft in the rock and cover you with my hand until I have passed by." Twice he's given the law and commandments engraved on tablets of stone.

Young David approaching the giant warrior, Goliath, with 5 smooth stones from the stream, and minstrels singing, "David triumphed over the Philistine with a sling and a stone." An older king David and the Psalmists, in songs of petition and praise, see safety and redemption in the rocky outcroppings, the hills and mountains.

Through the Song of Songs, the laments of Job, and the warnings of the prophets, these images are repeated. Isaiah reminds the people: "See, I lay a stone in Zion, a tested stone, a precious cornerstone for a sure foundation, the one who relies on it will never be stricken with panic."

Ezekiel brings the stones to life in a very personal way: "I will give you a new heart and put a new spirit in you; I will remove from you your heart of stone and give you a heart of flesh."

And in Jesus' teaching: "Which of you, if your son asks for bread, will give him a stone?" and, "Everyone who hears my words and puts them into practice is like a wise man who built his house on the rock."

Story upon story, generation upon generation, desert tribes and city dwellers, priests and prophets and poets, experiences of wellbeing and betrayal, exodus and promised land, are told through the artefacts of their time, the things found in their everyday lives: pebbles, stones, rocks, precious stones and gems.

What are we to make of all this? Can we reconcile, "Hear my prayer, answer me," with, "I trust you because you saved me?" Do we see ourselves as "living stones," being built into a spiritual house to be a holy priesthood? Do the images of a desert land far away speak to us of faith and safety? Or do they further confuse: all these concepts drawn on over the years by theologians and hymn writers and interpreters?

Cleft of the rock or barricade? Refuge and strength or stone to be hurled? Rock of ages or stumbling block? Stone wall or sanctuary? Stepping stone or Tombstone?

Theologian and educator Paul Tillich taught that several concepts that seem opposites of each other are instead in dynamic tension. Some such tensions include concepts such as order and chaos, being and becoming, freedom and destiny. Instead of trying to rationalize our way through this mishmash, this midrash, of metaphor, perhaps we can hold them in creative, dynamic tension—like the stones circles of Avebury and Aberdeenshire, the standing stones of Machrie Moor and Callenish, like the Ahu Tongariki (megaliths) of Rapa Nui and the medicine wheel of Big Horn, Wyoming—both the physical structures and their meaning have been built up by successive generations.

As we continue to do.

And there's another way to synthesize these apparent contradictions, and that's by letting them go; not thinking about them, but instead experiencing them in our bodies. Rev Jim Burklo asks: "What if your body rolled away the stone? What if your body walked out of the tomb?'

> (This section quotes from and adapts Jim Burklo's *Finding the Body* on the Progressive Christianity website.)

He invites us to meditate on the Easter story as if we are taking part in it... because feeling the story in our bodies teaches us to roll away the stones that hold us back from ways of living.

> "Pushing away the stone" is a metaphor that lives both in the muscles and in the mind... There's science behind this. The field of embodied cognition suggests that the metaphors we use in telling stories are based on our bodily experiences...

When we hear the story of the last supper, when Jesus breaks the bread, our mouths can salivate. We feel the weight of the tombstone against our shoulders. We sense the Galilee's water under our feet. We use our bodily sensations to think about abstract concepts. Neuroscience, cognitive psychology, and linguistics now suggest that our bodies take our myths literally… These stories… body and soul together, enabling us to change objective reality for the better… when we let the best stories of our tradition get into our muscles and train us to liberate each other into life. They happen in the present when we receive them into our being.

Close your eyes and relax. It's dark. It's silent. You are limp, unmoving. You were defeated, destroyed, ruined: crucified, dead, then buried.

That was then: and now is nothing—empty—still—lifeless. Your muscles aren't moving. Your mind is empty.

You stay like this for several minutes.

And now, just barely, you feel a tiny urge, just a little impulse… The urge gets stronger and stronger, the flame gets brighter and hotter inside of your body.

You feel it! You stand up and go to the stone that has sealed you in the dark tomb. You feel the stone against your hands, and you push; you lean into it with your chest and arms. You feel the weight, the pressure, in your upper body. Just as the stone begins to move, you open your eyes and see the light. You take a deep breath of the fresh air…"

When you're ready, come forward with the stone you're holding and add it to the cairn—of memories, of burdens to leave behind. Stones on the grave of a despair we can wake up from, reminders of the stories that have shaped us, symbolic peace treaties, paving for the paths we wish to take.

Bring your stone, add your own meaning, lay it down, build it up.

[Allow a space of silent time, while people add their stones to the cairn. When everyone is seated again, continue.]

It may be, when we've done all we can think of, it still feels as if we have a millstone around our neck; the cleft of the rock squeezing rather than sheltering; and the rock of ages too hard to be of comfort—there may be nothing left but to call, *O Lord, hear my prayer*—knowing that if we knock, we will be answered, if we hold out our hand, someone will take it; if we ask, we will receive.

So, our grieving can turn to grace. The weight of belief or disbelief is rolled away, and our guilt, unworthiness and failings are exposed as an empty cave, a place of darkness now lit by the knowledge, the faith, the conviction that we are safe, and worthwhile, and renewed.

Our stony, brittle, chipped hearts, our knocked-about-by-life confidence, can be exchanged for a new heart and a new spirit. The stone rejected because it doesn't seem to fit anywhere becomes the cornerstone, as we make meaning from our everyday, and build the sacred into the foundation and architecture of our lives.

So may it be.

Voices of the deep

A Reflection on sea-inspired stories and songs

Take a deep breath. Let it out.

Another. Smell the seawater, taste the salt. Let it go.

Close your eyes. Breathe in the tang, the heat, the brine.

See the waves, the driftwood, the wading birds. Feel the sand, hot underfoot, cool where wavelets creep up the beach.

Breathe freely and deeply. Inhale the memory of fish and sandcastles and kites and gulls and bonfires.

Sense the depths and currents. Feel the moon pull of tides.

Touch that space within you that yearns to return to the ocean where all life came from.

In *The Healing Moment*, Elizabeth Tarbox writes:

> "Each day I am newly reminded of my unworthiness—a dozen thoughts misspoken; another day when the good I do falls short of the good that I could do; myriad small interchanges; moments of sharing that strain to the breaking point my desire to be generous, helpful, and kind; months of careful work lost by a moment's impatience, a careless word.

> But when I am here at the edge of creation, breaking with the small tide over the sand, the need to do good rolls away; the question of what is right diminishes to insignificance and is easily borne away by the tiny waves. Here, where no words are spoken, none are misspoken.

> I am with the broken stubble of the marsh grass that holds on through the wrecking wind and the burning flood. I am with the grains that mould themselves around everything, accepting even so unworthy a foot as mine, holding and shaping it until it feels that it belongs.

> I stand somewhere between truth and vision, and what I don't know ceases to embarrass me, because what I do know is that the water feels gentle like a lover's touch, and the sand welcomes it.

> What I have done or failed to do has left no noticeable mark on creation. What I do or don't do is of no moment now. Now I am here and grateful to be touched, calmed, and healed by the immense pattern of the universe. And when I die, it will be an honour for my blood to return to the sea and my bones to become the sand.

> Reassured, I am called back to my life, to another day."

As inhabitants of an island nation, we in Aotearoa have sun, sand and sea in our veins. Our forebears came here via waka and sailing ship, and our celebration of the birth of Jesus brings a special gift to our summers.

Yet in the Hebrew scriptures, the sea is often a symbol of chaos, and in our hymn tradition, a metaphor for sin and despair. The ocean continues as the source of water, the source of life—and a place of danger. Liquefaction of sandy soil in Christchurch, devastating floods in Pakistan, oil spills and pollution in the Gulf of Mexico and in Nigeria, the melting icecaps threatening the millennia-old flow of the Gulf Stream—all remind us how dependent we are on water—and how we interfere with the ocean at our peril.

In our own place and time, we recall the tragedy of the *Wahine*, the sinking of the Lady Elizabeth II, the death of yachtsman Peter Blake at the hands of pirates, the young refugees from the *Tampa*, and the loss of 74 lives in Tongan waters in the *Princess Ashika*.

While preparing this service, I was flooded with memories of old hymns and fascinated by what inspired so many images of the sea, from "life's tempestuous sea," to "the moaning of the bar," from "wide, wide as the ocean," to "peace, be still," from the "ocean's depths," to "love lifted me," and "Will your anchor hold in the storms of life?"

Intriguingly, many lyricists refer to the ocean not just as the metaphorical location for present troubles but as a safe destination at the end of life. We can understand the 18th and 19th century preoccupation with death—shorter life expectancy, less reliable transportation, and lack of cures for fatal illness. Yet even contemporary writers like Colin Gibson offer images of leaving the coast and journeying to the rim of the sky and the sea… to eternity.

These voices from the deep remind us that life is a cycle, from the chaos of creation to the comfort of still waters, to rebirth as clouds and resurrection in rain, that what originates in the formless void eventually completes the circle in the waters of mother earth.

> The waves of the sea have lift up their voice,
> sore troubled that we in Jesus rejoice.
> The floods they are roaring, but Jesus is here.
> While we are adoring, he always is near.

Charles Wesley wrote *Ye Servants of God, Your Master Proclaim*, not as a hymn of praise but as encouragement for believers facing persecution. It appeared in 1744 in a small collection entitled *Hymns for Times of Trouble and Persecution* and was captioned "To be sung in tumult."

When devils engage, the billows arise,
and horribly rage and threaten the skies.
Their fury shall never our steadfastness shock—
the weakest believer is built on a rock.

It was a time of great tension in England, a time of bitter persecution for those new people called "Methodists." Mobs broke up their services, often hurling bricks, cabbages and eggs at the preachers. Undaunted, the Wesleys produced this collection of hymns to buoy their followers' spirits.

Sunset and evening star, and one clear call for me,
and may there be no moaning of the bar
when I put out to sea.

Alfred, Lord Tennyson wrote *Crossing the Bar* in his 81st year. A nurse who had been with him for 18 months suggested he turn his pen to writing hymns.

"Hymns are such dull things," he replied. But her suggestion evidently bore fruit.

In October 1889, with his son Hallam, Tennyson travelled from eastern England to his winter home on the Isle of Wight. As they crossed the Solent strait, the sounds of the sea and the phrase "moaning of the bar" kept running through Tennyson's mind and he jotted down some words to accompany it.

Hallam wrote: "After dinner he showed me the poem written out. I said, 'That is the crown of your life's work.' He answered, 'It came in a moment.' A few days before his death he said to me, 'Mind you, put *Crossing the Bar* at the end of all the editions of my poems.'"

In 1870, Edward Hooper became pastor of a small church in the New York harbour area, known as the Church of Sea and Land. It was while ministering at his sailor's mission in New York City that Edward Hopper wrote:

When the darkling heavens frown,
And the wrathful winds come down,
And the fierce waves, tossed on high,
Lash themselves against the sky,
Jesus, Saviour, pilot me,
over life's tempestuous sea.

Eternal Father, strong to save, written by William Whiting of Winchester, England, in 1860, was originally intended as a poem for a student of his, who was about to travel to the United States. This apparently traditional hymn is in fact extremely flexible. Because of its association with the US Navy, many extra verses have been added, to include Marines, Navy nurses and chaplains, SEALS and

Seabees, divers and submariners, the Antarctic and Arctic service, the Coast Guard—and many others.

In WWII, verses on naval aviation were written, and in the 20th century, space travel and exploration themes emerged, including a verse ending:

> O hear us when we seek Thy grace
> For those who soar through outer space.

Sadly, many of the extra verses feature forced rhymes and over-worked metaphor. As in many early hymns—and a distressing number of modern ones—trite lyrics are somewhat redeemed or at least disguised by the power and strength of the music. There's a treasure chest of stories about the tunes to these seafaring hymns as well, which we don't have time for today.

One final story of passion and redemption:

George Matheson was born in 1842 with only partial vision. He was a brilliant scholar and finished the University and the Seminary of the Church of Scotland with very high honours, helped by his sister, who learned Greek, Latin, and Hebrew to help him in his theological studies. His sight failed rapidly while at Glasgow University, and he became totally blind.

On the day of his sister's wedding, George Matheson—now in his 40s—was alone in his manse at Innellan; the rest of his family were staying in Glasgow. He wrote later, "Something happened to me, which was known only to myself, and which caused me the most severe mental suffering. The hymn was the fruit of that suffering."

It's believed the memory of his fiancée who left him just before their marriage, when she learned of his impending total blindness, prompted him—years later—to write of love that will not let me go:

> I trace the rainbow through the rain,
> And feel the promise is not vain
> That morn shall tearless be.

To conclude our reflection on the watery deeps and the creative impulses they inspire, here is not hymn lyrics but a story which takes us back to the seashore and the summer beach.

There are many versions of Loren Eiseley's story *The Star Thrower*, and like many parables and wisdom stories, it invites retelling:

> A man is walking along a beach where thousands of starfish have been washed up. He notices a boy picking up starfish one by one and throwing them back into the ocean. After a while, he asks the boy what he's doing. The boy replies that he's returning the starfish to the sea, otherwise they'll die.

The man asks how saving a few, when so many are doomed, would make any significant difference.

In reply, the boy picks up a starfish and throws it back into the ocean.

"Makes a difference to that one," he says.

May the mysteries of Sophia, the wise and playful Creator who is reflected in her creation, teach us to value her creatures and to live in right relationship with all of them, and with each other.

So may it be.

Affirmations, prayers, blessings

Blessings of Greenness

May the bright emerald of the Creator
the vivid lime inspiration of the Spirit
and the healing olive green of the One who showed the Way
bless you with summer in your heart
and inspire a spring in your step.

Go now in peace, to love and serve,
to plant and to reap,
to bless the earth with your hands.

Affirmation of Faith (ii): Come, let us walk the road

Come, let us walk the road that Sarai walked
leaving family, household and land
for a life in Canaan, promised to Abram.
Come, let us laugh with Sarah, prima gravida,
birthing a son, feeding incognito angels,
not knowing what the future holds.

Come, let us walk the road that Moses walked
stuttering before the blazing bush
jabbing the serpent-stick of faith into the desert ground
making holy the places where he stood
leading his people to a promised land.

Come, let us walk the road that Jesus walked
not sure what we are taking on
but leaving the familiar, whatever the cost
following a path of righteousness
and foolish loving
to birth a promised land.

Come, let us walk the path that spirals round
From Galilee to Jordan, Gethsemane to Golgotha
from land of milk and honey to kingdom come.

Litany for departing

We have brought our offerings of ourselves,
our symbols,
our personal meanings and intentions.

We have shared with each other
these wishes and burdens and gifts.

Let us now re-collect them
to weave them into the patchwork of our lives

to be part of the quilt we share with others
to warm their lives
and our world.

Walls, Gates and Tables

Leader:

When we would protect ourselves with walls
against others, and our own vulnerability.
When we would close our gates
to new possibilities and challenges in our lives.
When we would limit the numbers at our table
to those we know best, and are comfortable with—

All:

Instead let us open ourselves to the wonder of all creation:
welcome the gift of faith,
relax in the grace of rest,
lay down whatever burdens us.

Let us water the seedlings of wonder and possibility
for our own selves' healing
and the transformation of our world.

Amen

Trees blessing

And now, go in peace.

Stand tall as kauri
blossom bright as kōwhai
spread sheltering branches over those in need.

And may the fresh wild greenness of Creation
the vivid inspiration of Spirit
and the healing of the One
who walks the grass-lined ways of peace

refresh you, flower, and be alive in you
and those you love
this day and always

So may it be

Glossary and References

Glossary

Definitions of te reo Māori words are from the online Māori Dictionary and Te Ara: The Encyclopedia of New Zealand

Genderqueer: an umbrella term used to describe identities outside the gender binary... Genderqueer can be used to describe a non-binary identity, but it can also encompass fluidity in gender identity or expression. Where queer is an umbrella term that includes all sexual orientations other than heterosexual, genderqueer refers to gender identities that are not aligned with the gender binary—www.verywellmind.com

Koan: A paradox to be meditated upon that is used to train Zen Buddhist monks to abandon ultimate dependence on reason and to force them into gaining sudden intuitive enlightenment—Merriam Webster Dictionary

Midrash: the attempt to penetrate the spirit of the [First Testament] text, to examine the text from all sides, to derive interpretations not immediately obvious, to illuminate the future by appealing to the past.—The Jewish Encyclopaedia

Mana: prestige, authority, control, power, influence, status, spiritual power, charisma—mana is a supernatural force in a person, place or object.

mana ōrite: equality

mana tangata whenua: indigenous rights

manaakitanga: hospitality, kindness, generosity, support—the process of showing respect, generosity and care for others.

mōhiotanga: knowledge, knowing, understanding, comprehension, intelligence, awareness, insight, perception

murunga hara: forgiveness

tātou tātou e: "all of us, all of us"

Te Tiriti o Waitangi: The Treaty of Waitangi, New Zealand's founding document, was meant to be a partnership between Māori and the British Crown. However, different understandings of the treaty, and breaches of it, have caused conflict.

wairua: spirit, soul - spirit of a person which exists beyond death. It is the non-physical spirit, distinct from the body and the *mauri*. To some, the *wairua* resides in the heart or mind of someone while others believe it is part of the whole person and is not located at any particular part of the body

Wairua Tapu: Holy Spirit

whakamatau: to attempt, try, experiment, cause to know, teach, tempt, try out, trial

whare karakia: church (building), synagogue, house of prayer—a building for religious services

Bibliography and sources

Armstrong, Karen, *A History of God,* London: Vintage, 1999 (first pub. Heinemann 1993)

Buber, Martin, "Plato and Isaiah" and "False Prophets" in *Essays on the Bible,* New York: Schocken Books, 1982 in RELI 209 Course Notes reading 12

Cohen, Leonard. *Treaty*—CD *You want it darker* (2016)

Coombs, Jessie. *Thoughts for the Inner Life* reproduced by Ulan Press (2012) originally published before 1923

Farrington, Tim. *The Monk Downstairs*. HarperOne (2006)

Geering, Lloyd, *Tomorrow's God,* 1994, NZ: Bridget Williams Books

Humphries, Pat. (1984) *Never Turning Back* recorded by Judy Small on "One Small Voice in a Crowd" (1985) © Crafty Maid Music

Maniapoto, Moana. *Treaty*—Moana and the Moa Hunters, CD *Rua* (1998)

Spong, John Shelby, *Rescuing the Bible from Fundamentalism,* 1991, HarperSanFrancisco

Swimme, Brian. *Universe Is a Green Dragon: A Cosmic Creation Story*. Bear & Company (1984)

Ward, James, "The Context of the Prophetic Message" in *Thus Says the Lord,* Nashville: Abingdon Press, 1982 in RELI 209 Course Notes reading 13

Thanks

To all who bought my books, *You who delight me* and *Something new to say*, for your encouragement to keep writing and sharing worship resources and to ordained and lay worship leaders who're using these liturgies to nurture inclusive, progressive faith communities.

Thank you again to these faith communities:

GalaXies (gay, lesbian, bisexual, transgender Christians and their families and friends) spiritual community

Ephesus Group, Wellington

and especially

St Andrew's on The Terrace Presbyterian Church

for whom most of these prayers, reflections and blessings were written and presented.

Thank you always

to my husband, Warwick Metcalfe—for support and love

to my daughter Lauren Angela White, for inspiration and shining brilliantly in my life

and to our darling grandsons, Luka and Alexei, who made me fall in love all over again

Also by bronwyn angela white

something new to say:
words of spirit, faith and celebration for Advent and Christmas

2nd edition
Published: 2022
B/W text, 70pp
Soft cover
ISBN: 9781991027368

This collection celebrates a festive season where pohutukawa and rata are in bloom, friends gather around barbecues or picnic at the beach on Christmas Day, and many people travel to catch up with family or enjoy school holidays.

The prayers, affirmations, reflections, and blessings are in inclusive language, with an emphasis on "faith not belief" and social justice. This book is ideal for progressive and liberal faith communities and churches.

Print books and eBook editions available at
www.philipgarsidebooks.com

www.ingramcontent.com/pod-product-compliance
Lightning Source LLC
Chambersburg PA
CBHW070933120626
46546CB00004B/1404